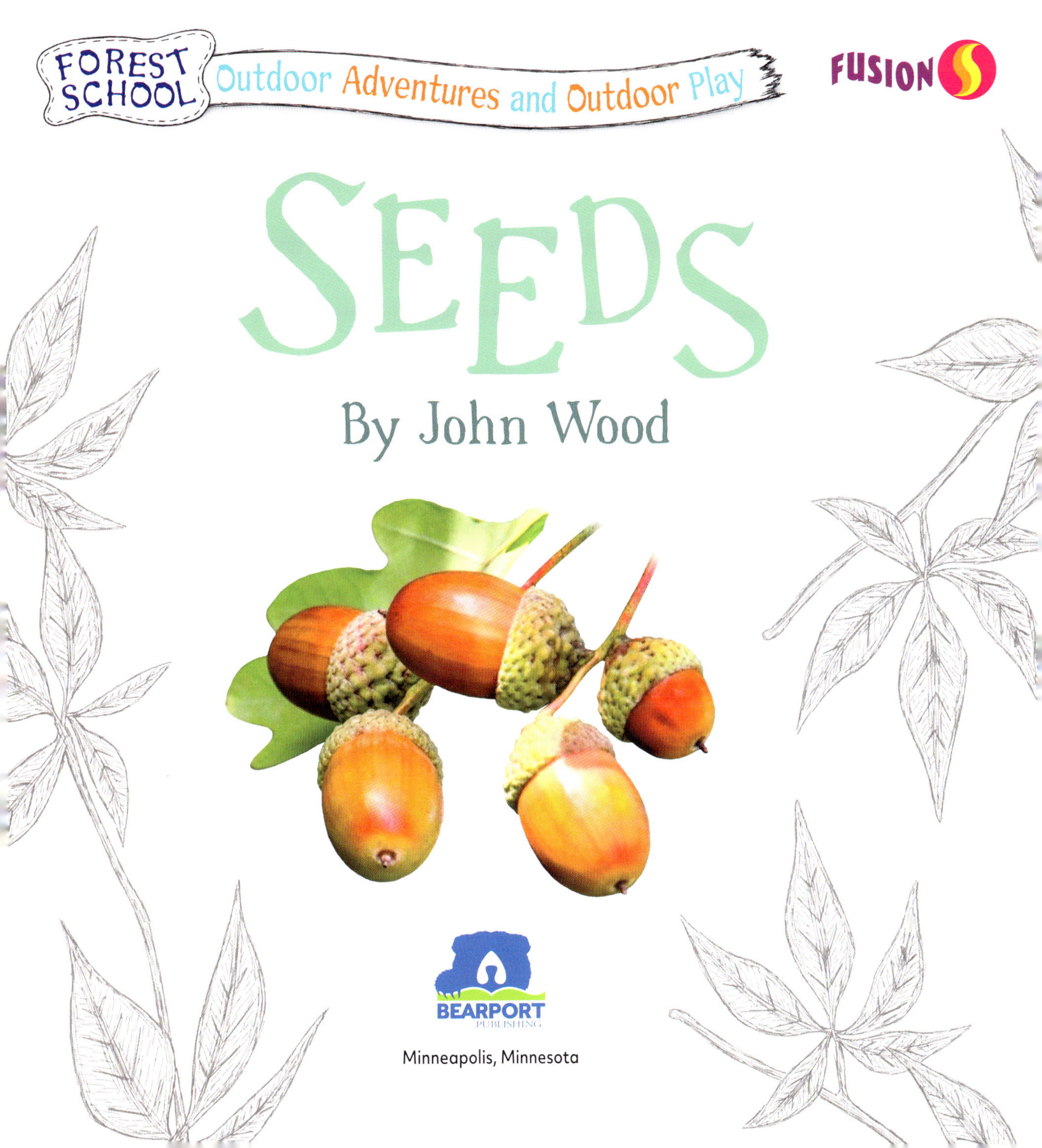
FOREST SCHOOL
Outdoor Adventures and Outdoor Play
FUSION
SEEDS
By John Wood
BEARPORT
PUBLISHING
Minneapolis, Minnesota

Credits:
Front Cover – SakSa, Samuel Borges Photography, Lotus Images, 4&5 – Lars Schmidt-Eisenlohr, AmeliaFox/iStock, 6&7 – Erikka pics, Monkey Business Images, 8&9 – Sergey Novikov, hadynyah/iStock, 10&11 – KLYONA, Tracy Immordino, Sabino Parente, RG-ve, Vova Shevchuk, Dionisvera, 12&13 – scooperdigital, jjMiller11/iStock, 14&15 – redmal/iStock, Paladin12/iStock, 16&17 – Alena Levykin, Valentyn Volkov, Maxim Aksutin, 18&19 – RedHelga/iStock, gresei, Andrei Dubadzei, SThofanM, raditya, Chamois huntress, AK-Media, 20&21 – Shestakoff, Heike Rau, AnnGaysorn, 22&23 – MJfotografie.cz, imtmphoto. Images are courtesy of Shutterstock.com. With thanks to Getty Images, Thinkstock Photo, and iStockphoto.

Library of Congress Cataloging-in-Publication Data is available at www.loc.gov or upon request from the publisher.

ISBN: 978-1-63691-465-7 (hardcover)
ISBN: 978-1-63691-472-5 (paperback)
ISBN: 978-1-63691-479-4 (ebook)

For more information, write to Bearport Publishing, 5357 Penn Avenue South, Minneapolis, MN 55419. Printed in the United States of America.

CONTENTS

Welcome to the Forest

Welcome to forest school. Let's explore, play, and create!

Step outside into a great big classroom full of plants. These plants grow seeds. Then, the seeds turn into more plants!

Taking Care of Nature

Any time we go into **nature**, we must take care of it. We should leave the forest as we found it.

Stay on the path during forest school. That way, we won't hurt any plants or animals. What else can we do to care for the forest?

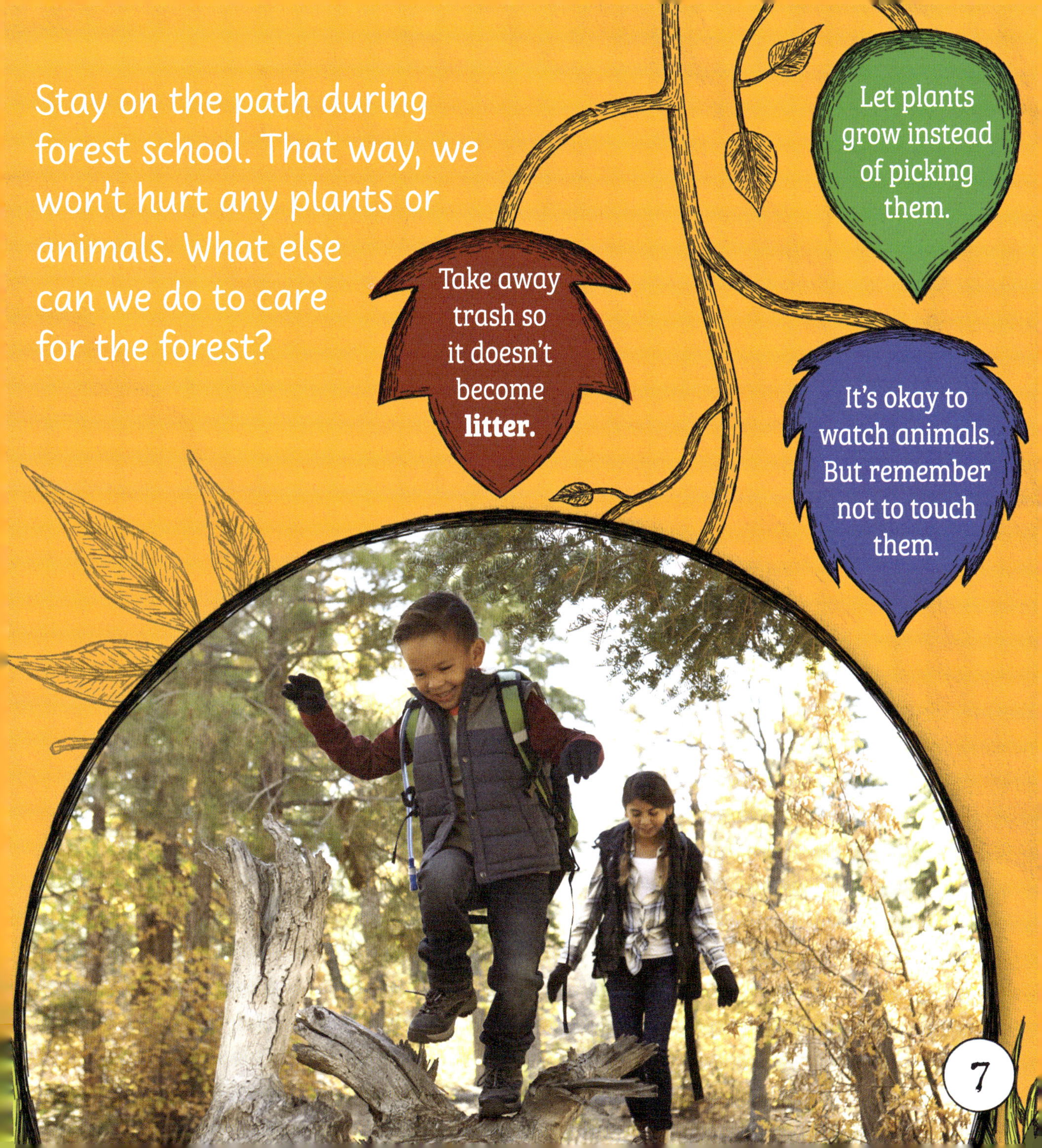

SEARCHING FOR SEEDS

Almost every plant in the forest began as a seed. Seeds can be different sizes, shapes, and colors. Let's find as many as we can!

Some seeds grow in fruit. This includes apple seeds and peach pits. Seeds also grow in flowers and pine cones.
A coconut is actually a very big seed!

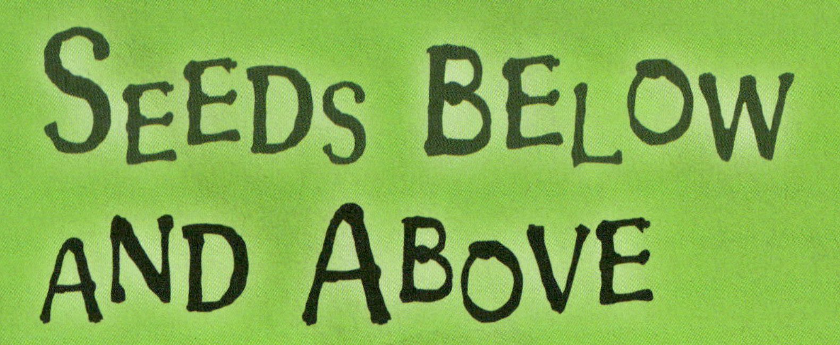

Seeds Below and Above

If you look closely, you can find seeds all around the forest. Which seeds are growing near the ground?

Grass seeds

Thistle seeds

Dandelion seeds

Now, look up into the trees.
Where are the seeds hiding?
Never eat seeds or fruit that you find in the forest. They might make you sick.
These seeds come from maple trees.
Acorns are the seeds of oak trees.
Holly trees grow red berries with seeds inside.

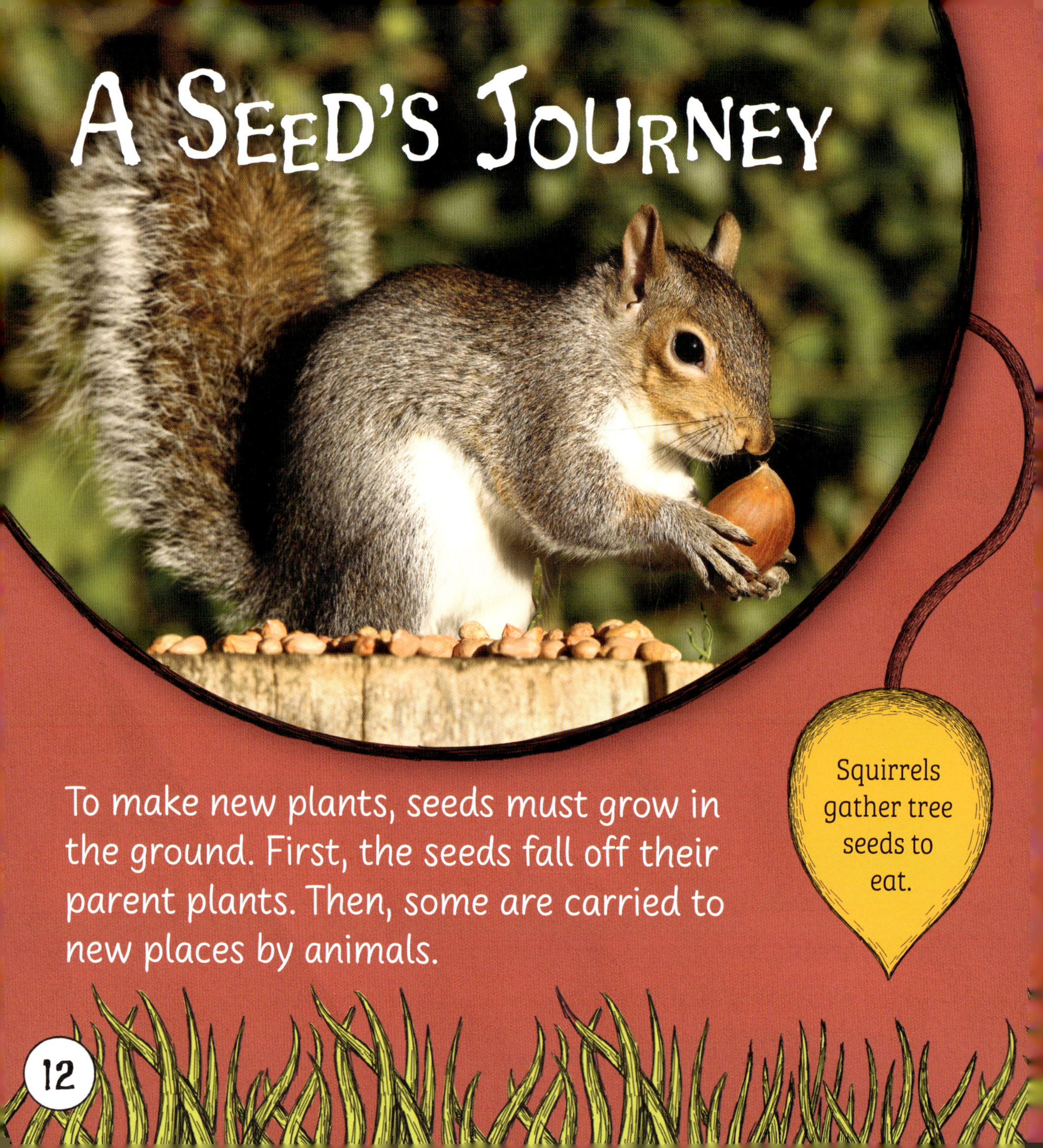

A Seed's Journey

To make new plants, seeds must grow in the ground. First, the seeds fall off their parent plants. Then, some are carried to new places by animals.

Squirrels gather tree seeds to eat.

Seeds can also be moved around by wind. Once a seed **settles** somewhere on the ground, it can start to grow into a new plant.

Some animals eat seeds. Then, they poop them out in new places.

Growing Up

How does a seed grow into a new plant? First, **roots** grow out of the seed.

Plants need sunlight to grow.

Then, the roots get water and **nutrients** from the **soil**. This helps the seed grow a **shoot** that pops out of the ground. And the tiny plant keeps growing!

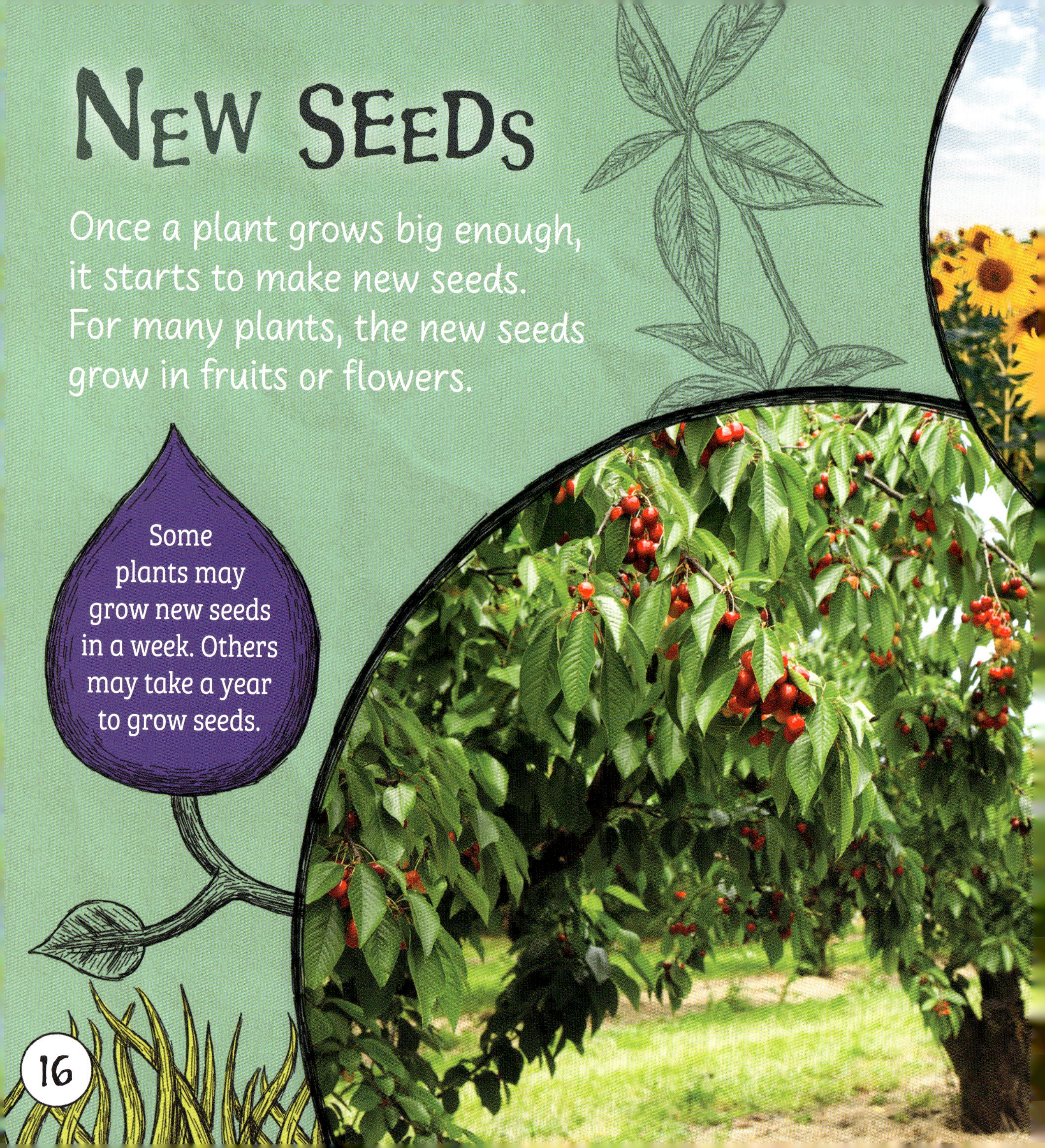

New Seeds

Once a plant grows big enough, it starts to make new seeds. For many plants, the new seeds grow in fruits or flowers.

Some plants may grow new seeds in a week. Others may take a year to grow seeds.

Fruits and flowers can become food for birds, bees, and butterflies.

Did you know that most nuts are actually seeds? Some grow inside fruit. Can you match these nuts to the trees they make?

Pine tree
Cocoa tree
Almond tree

GET MAKING!

Do you want to try growing plants at home? You can grow seeds from fruit you eat or buy some seeds at the store.

Place your seeds in soil. Give them water and sunlight. Then, watch them grow!
Make seed bombs that grow lots of flowers.
Mix flower seeds, clay soil, and **compost** to make the seed bombs. Then, put them in the ground so the flowers can grow.

Time To Think

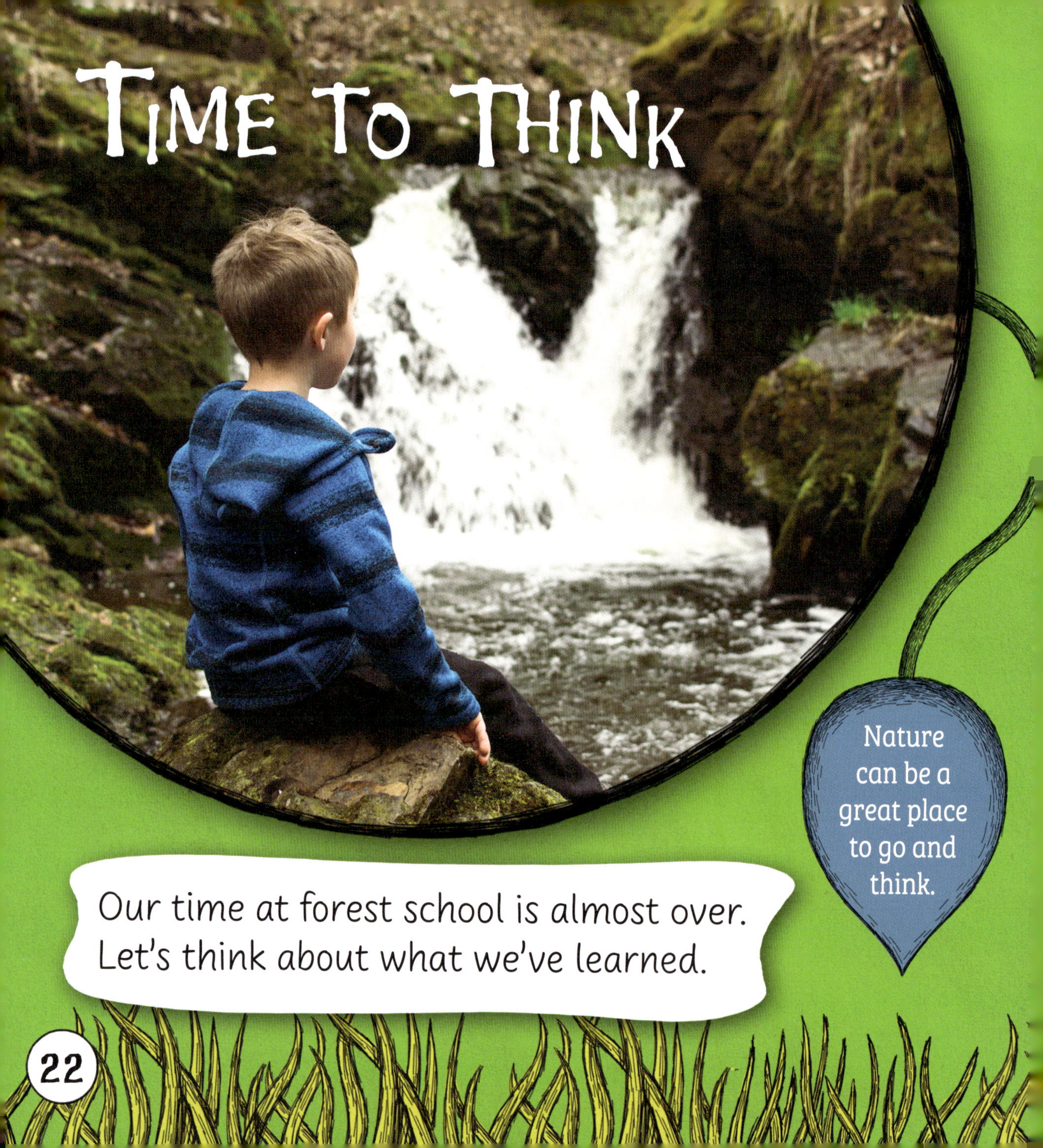

Nature can be a great place to go and think.

Our time at forest school is almost over. Let's think about what we've learned.

What did you learn about seeds? And how did learning about nature make you feel?
What do you want to explore next time at forest school?

Glossary

compost material made of rotted plants and food that can be used to make soil better

litter things that have been thrown away and are lying on the ground

nature the world and everything in it that is not made by people

nutrients natural things that plants, animals, and people need to live and grow

roots the parts of a plant that grow underground

settles stays in place

shoot the part of a new plant that is just starting to grow above the ground

soil dirt that plants grow in

Index

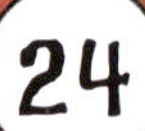